BLACK METAMORPHOSES

Sometimes you have to reach far and wide to get at the truth. The reaching is the "birthing [of a] new alphabet for desire." Shanta Lee is in search of that new language, an unbroken path to the truth. Inspired by Ovid, her *Black Metamorphoses* fuses new poetry with old forms to make things right through needful change. The travesty of slavery and the discovery of hope "bring us nectar that bathes wounds." Read this book and be dazzled into a new way of seeing.

—Pablo Medina, *Foreigner's Song: New and Selected Poems*

Starting before Eve, Shanta Lee's collection, *Black Metamorphoses*, begins with an earnest desire to know what will be buried in us, in our blood. What is left in the wake of our hunger? What myths travel the wind, expand, implode, pull us in? Lee sees gods reincarnate everywhere and paints them anew, haints in the garden, in the copper, in a leather purse, even "These fingernails filled with Black body" are illumined herein. *Black Metamorphoses* posits that Black folks are nearly invincible, eternal. Despite what we carry and how far, we'll keep on living.

—Remica Bingham-Risher, *Soul Culture: Black Poets, Books, and Questions that Grew Me Up*

I hesitate to call any work of contemporary poetry an *epic* but no other word will describe Shanta Lee's *Black Metamorphoses*. Lee is an audacious mythmaker, inspired by Ovid but also keen to debunk the Eurocentric patriarchy that he represents. In a series of wildly ambitious and formally inventive monologues and character studies, Lee offers a searing threnody for the victims of slavery and the African Diaspora. Yet the book is also a moving and hard-won celebration of the black body: the rituals of mourning give way to empowerment. As she writes in one poem, "It be both crown and burden,/ glory of yours and grievance of othas/ Be not touched by jus any hands,/ it be bridge to your making or the road to a bound soul." *Black Metamorphoses* is a stunning accomplishment.

—David Wojahn, *From the Valley of Making: Essays on the Craft of Poetry (Poets On Poetry)*

BLACK METAMORPHOSES

Shanta Lee

etruscan press

Etruscan Press
Wilkes University
84 West South Street
Wilkes-Barre, PA 18766
(570) 408-4546

www.etruscanpress.org

Published 2023 by Etruscan Press
Printed in the United States of America
Cover art: *Tereus, Procne, and Philomela's Children*, 2021 © Alan Blackwell
Cover design by Logan Rock
Interior design and typesetting by Jason Miller
The text of this book is set in Adobe Garamond Pro.

Second Edition

17 18 19 20 5 4 3 2 1

Library of Congress Cataloging-in-Publication Data

Names: Gander, Shanta Lee, 1978- author.
Title: Black metamorphoses / Shanta Lee Gander.
Description: Second edition. | Wilkes-Barre, PA : Etruscan Press, 2023. | Summary: "Black Metamorphoses pierces a 2,000+ year-old veil inspired by a range of Ovidian myths while resisting a direct conversion of the work. This collection explores the Black psyche, body, and soul, through inversion and brazen confrontation of work that has shaped Western civilization. In a poetic range of forms, voices, and rhythms, the reader is bathed in ancestral memory, myth, and sense of the timeless of the shapeshifting, resilient Black body"-- Provided by publisher.
Identifiers: LCCN 2021053881 | ISBN 9781736494660 (paperback ; acid-free paper)
Subjects: LCSH: Blacks--Poetry. | LCGFT: Poetry.
Classification: LCC PS3607.A4416 B57 2023 | DDC 811/.6--dc23/eng/20211105
LC record available at https://lccn.loc.gov/2021053881

Please turn to the back of this book for a list of the sustaining funders of Etruscan Press. This book is printed on recycled, acid-free paper.

"There are years that ask questions and years that answer."
Zora Neale Hurston, *Their Eyes Were Watching God*

"You wanna fly, you got to give up the shit that weighs you down."
Toni Morrison, *Song of Solomon*

"No one knows the precise birthdate of African America.

Perhaps no one is supposed to know. African America is like the enslaved woman who tragically never knew exactly when she was born. African America is like the enslaved man who chose his own birthday—August 20, 1619—based on the first record of a day when people of African descent arrived in one of the thirteen British colonies that later became the United States."

Four Hundred Souls, **Ibram X. Kendi and Keisha N. Blain (editors)**

To all bodies and bones forcibly travelled.
May you root. May you dig in without apology.

TABLE OF CONTENTS

 **BOOK I**

 BOOK II

BOOK III

BOOK IV

BOOK V

ACKNOWLEDGEMENTS AND GRATITUDE

My thanks to *NOMBONO: An Anthology of Speculative Poetry* by Sundress Publications for publishing "The Return of Hyena Man."

My gratitude to…

Parneshia Jones, David Wojahn, and Philip Metres. You all were my poetry guides for this work at VCFA. My thanks to my extended VCFA family for adding to the depth of my writing life.

My growing community of fellow creative misfits which includes many, you all know who you are.

My boundless depth of gratitude to artist extraordinaire, Alan Blackwell. My thanks to you and especially your beautiful family for supporting your work on this project. Your art opened new dimensions to this text while also illustrating the many hours, days, emotional and physical engagement that you dedicated to my work. I am in awe and appreciation.

And my expression of thanks would not be complete without acknowledging the 2000+ year old phone line opened to Ovid.

In the Beginning…

That hunger? Thirst? Lust? Want?   *?*
                   ?   *? And*   *?*

No letters contained
what was about to happen

My bones, travelled ragged
Tongue twisted, torn   Gone

Body, unburied
They said this is where the feva started

Thirst unquenched

The way to Mama's place is fuzzy
They teach me coordinates to a new place

Was I Mitochondrial Eve's cursed brood?

They said I could learn to speak like them
If I be and do, then I too could…

BOOK I

Two questions that can only be answered one way:
Are you dreaming?
Are you awake?

No

Hunger like her mama
Most strong in white gaze as in
a Cowbird's flirtation
Sprouted in eyes to tongues
to bellies pregnant with stolen milk
to restless hands
These fingernails filled with Black body,
scrapin to get back to forgotten

Here, the Gods of this
New World demanded…

Erysichthon's Seed

Before, Brown bodies dealt in
Brown bodies. Before the Portuguese
Before, Europe knew little bout Black…
how it lingers on the tongue

Erysichthon pulled Hunger
out of his bowels figurin,
If I can't soothe her, I'll marry her
We can eat the world together

Eyes taste beginning, make new words
Hands taste bodies, make new narrative
Black bodies…a synonym for Empire

They birthed many…Ark of Agony,
Ocean, Hunger, Terra…Balm

Equiano tells the tale, *Captain threatens to eat me…*
Vanished bodies continue to tell…
from Lion Mountains to Roar of Thunder
to Land of Burnt Face to Corridor
of Camps   these be Ministers of Destruction

Merchants of Doom, Soul Carriers, Flesh Mongers,
He-Who-Butchers-Bodies,
Demons of Desolation,
Priests of Wreckage, Flesh Eaters,
Magicians…

The stories remain in the bones
of bodies blessed Black. Equiano
said what others said what Geronimo warned:
White eyes, they speak hunger
White eyes, they be danger

Ark of Agony fed on howls, screams &
stench…his empty-bellyful needs more bodies
The Demons of Desolation steal more bodies

From oil to anything, barnacles scraped, candle wax
to leather…this crew of *Peggy*, that crew
of France's *Tyger*, others on Nantucket's *Essex*
knew the rule: *What's at sea stays at sea.*
When all fails at sea, fake a draw to decide
When all fails, feed from a stolen body

8

Ocean swallowed the unwanteds
He took children, he took women, swallowed
the old, swallowed infants, ate the sick, mouth
opened wide to all who said they'd fly back

But bones don't stop singing,
sing loudest in water
Black bodies became Whale Fall
Those bones be the Bimini road
from there to here

Lilburn's playscape, betta than a formal ball
Black body wonderland, body bound to plank,
fire high ax in hand. Others chose urge
at arm length, handcuff 'em to a bedpost
Others chose to feed bodies to the Cotton Jinn

Terra stretched across the New World
rivaling her brothers and sisters
Necks, knuckles, limbs of all kinds
Skin, scalps, skulls, blood. Most preferred?
A Feast of Flayed Men
that rivaled Aztec tradition
Skin as shoes
Skin as money purse
Skin, the inheritance given to white children

Leather Face be no fiction but old deity
Leather Face one of the Eternal Hungry
A sacrifice to shallow graves of many bodies,
bodies of no bury. Nat Turner and Sam Hose,
constellation points to all the othas
Taste turned unstoppable cuz...
We can dine on Black bodies for generations

Balm took no form, endless appetite like her kin
Took anything in the ministry of feel good:
Human fat to soothe the bruise
A mortar pestled skull to dull a head's ache,
King's drops with wine or chocolate,
Mommy's helper turned mummy fever

Human flesh to tongue to cure? Nothin new
Appetites be not created. Crave be groomed

Somethin bout diamonds, rubber, cocoa
Somethin bout cotton, copper, tin, tea, and all them spices
Unbroken from the boy somewhere in Texas in 2016…he tells the class,
I've got a leather purse made of Black skin
Gotten from great grand to grand to papa, soon it'll be his
Man handin hunger to man forgettin why they were trynna
get back to Gods of names forgotten

Invoking seasoning, adding years, feeding tongues to language
Hang a live Black body in a smoke house or a kitchen
Use pepper
Use salt
Add vinegar
Add coal oil
Add some turpentine…
Whatever will do for a Black body
Whatever is sanctioned from the Old World

Hunger left Erysichthon,
birthed the twins Lust and Appetite on her own

They wanna know,
you got room for what tickles your tongue?

Black body,
no silent cuisine,

Black body demands,
You got room for   in your belly?

"People ██████████████ take
████████████ realize ████████
███████████████████████████

—their ██████████
██████████, legacy."

Tereus, Procne, and Philomela's Children (Part I)

You beat me blind with the devil's claw
    you call a switch as if chasing a spirit

As if trying to return to that place
    we can't name. Opportunity's caravan

bound displaced souls
    with Spanish moss while the South's light

laid imprint upon ears. Blue bottled
    haint trees translate windpipes, chimes eluding

twined tongues humming Mahalia Jackson,
    grits, that plant that'll make a man leave

Hats never kiss beds while burnt hair,
    some Blue Magic, and Mama's hot comb

fills nostrils and stomachs with hope,
    a bridge of return to that place

of lost memory, the missing coils twisted
    wit butter knives among the amnes'd…no rise,

acceptance neva given
    Chanting hexabys, refusing the dreamin

Tasting like Sa calling
    Alatangana's children carryin

collisions of Mama,
    French, Papa, Dutch, Sista, English, and Brotha's tongues

Swallowing wind, rinsing with wake disintegrating
    home...we be in Wander's

amniotic sac. Motion's the caul
    that tried to cling to our faces,

bodies but we be born of air
    defyin nets, sky as if tryin...

We tell our children,
    Follow the fallen feathers. Find that place.

Echo's Revenge

How far would you go to answer Hunger?
   Crave?
      This exhibit is about Desire

I.

Tea, silk, spice, lacquer, and,   ,
      and,   , was worth the orgasm of trespass

A birthmark of lust that still haunts
      the face of the gas station attendant

II.

Along the slippery slope of consent
      a man explains,

Some things are worth stealing

to a woman whose bones ask,
      Who is the thief?

III.

Benin bronze, Lost-Stolen-Friend Denied
      a Passage Home, Papyrus of Ani

180,000 Cameroon,
      75,000 Madagascar

add up to more and denial
   Stolen solace of stolen bones

thrown by no hand from an Indiana
   Farmhouse to unmarked graves

to Godhood on canvases
   birthing new alphabet for desire

Would I?

IV.

Keep livin they say, Mama said,
   Auntie said. It's the only way to answer

what can't be...suppose we all became
   Paris—it can't be desire if we can't name our price

Can't be called desire if it's not worth war

V.

Follow the footprints of want around
   the world, go where lust has struck,

wander past where they've hung the bodies,
   past old China looming out of place,

enter a hall. Look between
   the partitions, the white space. Look there.

Look for...

Poisonwell Diaries:
Hades and Persephone in the New World

I.

Unsee you,
unfeel?
I can't

You, stolen by my hands. Me,
        doing a king's bidding. Both of us far from home

A comparison without a difference
        Still…you be like first feeling

of home. I risked our children's children's ire
        and shame upon my soul

I ask all futures from my loins   forgive me
        I am blessed you'd have me. What is owned

when a heart's ensnared? They all say—
        this is ungodly, my heart's hunger

like that of Byblis and Myrrha
        risking blood bond   I burn hotter

How can love be legislated?
        Many moons from now, they gonna say you had no say

They gonna say this is rape.
        This relationship won't exist on its own terms within no time

Alas, they were never here
        They don't know the weight of such things

II.

Bits and pieces of the story went that way
Mama sold, Papa the kind so good, a prized stud
My blood sprinkled on every plantation
I wonder if tastebuds started at the bosom I was denied?

Were othas like me?

He said this be different
I say no man just gonna come take,
but this…this be no theft. This kinda taken had a lettin
Ya'll love Love forgettin her provenance
be straight outta starvation and abundance
Want ain't even coverin it

More like   Crave

More like no letters can arrange themselves for that kinda…
More like the sun rising early to catch a glimpse of the moon
only to burn the rays that remind us of a yearnin not soothed
So it is, no and mine resides beyond my skin

So it is. This be no romance.
You must answer to your own Gods for that
And so it is, for treatin me like your Persephone,
you must ansuh to my people. Talk to my Gods
about this throne you offer in the land of Jangare
where the pomegranate stained even my lips

How much more you got to quench what I need?

Poisonwell Diaries:
The Mistress

Unrooted. My tongue?
Torn, disremembered
Intimacy blooms
in this asylum

Some say sin
I say full
fingertips first unwanted

A paved road to a possible beating,
started as a game as girls
Ignorin our mamas warnins, ignorin our stations

Hers, the big house,
as in inheritor of all this
My place, the cabins

We bear our skin
They say she owns me
They don't know, I own her

She licks her lips,
drags eyes slow
from my toes to my hair strand

fingertips followed by hands
going where her father tries to go
She dared me silent

Hands followed yanked body behind
the tree, into the barn,
into her bed before sunrise

Want knew no bounds,
but want must be bargained
Save me from your daddy, it's yours

Save me from the beatings, it's yours
Save me from what all this is…
I'm yours beyond body

Her smell,
her desire?
Now my own

She had to marry
I came along
as wedding gift

It's been a spell
His body's in the cellar
They all say we unspeakable,

but this nectar bathes wounds
This…this kinda feel good can't be twisted into they kinda wrong

Poisonwell Diaries:
The Ghost

Mama birthed me, Papa sold me in the land of weeping willows
Traces of sin trail miles across skin, I go by Never Forget
My body's evidence of daddy's pestilence spread across the land

His sin traces my skin, a path never forgotten
Nameless, nationless, I root where I am thrown
Centuries of science bloom from my womb, I be the world's original balm

Without name, without place, I root at my command
My children captured, bound, and tricked…they only see this path
Your price placed pon this body, but my soul's my own

Thefted bodies be not yours, bound mouths can't speak *Yes*
My grandchildren no longer tricked destroyed their footprints pon this path
Your babies knew my nipple well, it's what made me owned

Yet this kidnapped body be not yours, I neva gave you all this
An American nightmare of your making, unbroken beginning tethered to time
Your grand babies etched my body sayin it was theirs to own

A nightmare you crafted with lineage bound, souls tethered
My children's children know the truth: You are because you took
In this land of possession, can you stay fed on snatched and looted?

My body bred many, memory embosses this land
Our children's children's children tell the tale   *Some debts can't be paid*
Dismember the archive, imbibe this truth,

      Mama, who is she? Papa raped me and sold me down the river
      I slit my throat and papa's too to haunt this land of weeping willows

BOOK II

Energy is neither created nor detroyed
First Law of Thermodynamics

Energy, like the Black body, can shapeshift
Addendum to the First Law of Thermodynamics

Atlas? What About the Rainbow Serpent?

Something about Hercules joining
caused Atlas to shift his burden of punishment
Something like daddy issues, mommy issues,
a Greek man's burden. I heard of a Rainbow Serpent
holding not just an edge, but all of creation along
with looted bodies from there to here, here   and here
Scattered like seed. How long can a tail be held
by the tip in one's own mouth? Talk about burden,
how long can one body bend to hold stolen children?
The weight of the bones, original names, and

If You End Up in Jangare:
An Incantation for Remembering

As creators go,

they got it wrong
> bodies fashioned by an African woman

As creation goes,
> a conversation turned echo of a Mama

making sure her children find home
> Before echo be incantation

blessing the bodies gone missing
> in the world of spirits, in Jangare

Hair

upon your head
> transmuting bodies from stolen to freedom

All togetha, a reminder of the untamed,
> single strand full of life's essence

It be both crown and burden,
> glory of yours and grievance of othas

Be not touched by jus any hands,
> it be bridge to your making

or the road to a bound soul

Because they be

world, because they be Maat of Truth
        and Judgement, because they be

power and passion, encompassing
        gaze and glare bringin whole bodies to God of Succumb

Because they be piercer of veil,
        the touch without hand, they be your gift of shapeshift

They be not windows. They are shutters.

The mouth

as doorway for the way
        it will be pried open, for the way

witch's bridles will try to block temptation
        For the way it gifts sleep and wake

with mere kiss. Let it guard rooted muscle of taste. Let it
        guard the sire of curses and blessings

Let it guard the gateway of life force…

The throat

that be bridge between body
        and world, bridge between known of home

and amnesia of New World encased in story
        Between that which flowers and grows

unfurling upon tongue into world, that
     which be imitated

neva embodied by the mimicrian
     The throat that be the ferry between

Shadowlands and Land of Sunshine

Let body

be filled with a heart
     in balance with Maat's feather, that which be

seat of rhythm, of movement
     Seat of making and unmaking of universe,

seat of source, the cor in courage
     Let this drive the move and groove of hips child

as in dance as in Gnostic speak as in,
     To the universe belongs the dancer

…for they who do not dance will not know what happens.

Be this a body

of limbs to create
     civilization. Be this

a body indigestible by Saturn's
     endless belly, be this a body

that Hunger has not the space to hold,

be this a body with the bones that vibrate

inscribed with rebellion,
        flight, and your secret names

Be this a body covered…wizened with…

Fill with blood

that be lineage,
        fill with drink of the mystics that be milk

of life, fill with the dew of Mama
        that be the walk between worlds, the kind of blood

that be the birth of names,
        Elixir, Ambrosia,
        Drink of Most Holy

Your body

in the Valley of the Lost
        A body dismembered refusing dismemberment,

reappeared as witness, etched archive
        sprouted from scattered seed reminding Home

of what has gone. Your soul Lazarus,
        your body   The resting note,

the reminder

        You Are Mine

Africa's Dream

On she went, on she bragged
until I interrupted her ass
That may be your doom, said I,
there are worse fates than birthing a continent,

or brightening a galaxy
Those I saw, not two, not three,
but a table of them crowdin me. Not sure if I stood,
not sure if I laid, one thing felt certain,
my body became their display

Enter a lion, mighty and strong
He gave a new name from Cape of Storms to Cape of Hope
Enter another lion, this one stronger than the last
As parts of me gone missin neva to be retrieved
He laid his paw upon me sayin, *Power is money.*

Money is power...we can't achieve anything without it

He said I'd remain his child, he'd let me roam within the confines of home
from Cape Town to Cairo. So many entered I lost count
Another lion declared his share. He made no deals,
made no promises—said I owed him for what he offered

He vowed to take my hands, feet, otha limbs if need be
His greed like all the others, his greed an endless pit
Enter an eagle claimin his due, argue or challenge?
I didn't dare. He gifted me poisoned wells, bridges to nowhere
He took my children as if lives to spare. This eagle starved me

Another strolled in boldly…this one wanted more children
Unnoticed nor forgotten, a rooster and two wolves. The rooster lacked power,
the rooster lacked glory, but employed cunning like the others
He paid my family no cows, no money. He paid no goats   I paid the dowry
I rivaled the bride of the Robber Bridegroom,

these creatures be my doom

Two eagles
Two wolves
A rooster
Three lions

a bear, a dragon   all seeking their share

They wanted my jewels, wanted my oils, got drunk off my cocoa
Took my fabric, stole my tea and tin. Who knows what else is missing
now that they've stormed in?
Their hunger turned madness the way blood spilled

Not sure if I stood, not sure if I laid…

More than two countries fought ovah me
I be not porcelain. I be not fair. About these facts, they did not care
In this dream, many kingdoms in my womb
In this dream, my body and spirit fill the world as if mere room

I be bride as in the tie that bound us all,
the thread within humanity's lace
Europa, unlike you, I know my dream was no mistake
I saw traders turned missionaries turned merchants then soldiers

I jolted awake unable to shake that sound, the beat,

that thump,
the strum,
a particular hum,
a sound I carry from sleep to wake to the edge of dream
it refuses to leave my bones

Hermaphroditus Tells It

There's a part of the story neva told
a truth about the price paid for askin Gods
to bring bodies together like dat. Spoken
in a state of dat kinda depthless thirst,
madness even! The bigger cost in
proceedin to will that kinda want
from impatient unanswered prayer—

Warn your children's children's children's children,
tell them about that time. That time when...

The Witness Tree

I ain't no double-headed kind
I don't get drunk off they symbols
That's how you get got in the land of spirits
They first break your tongue,
piece it together in they own
I see beyon eyes, listen beyon ears
Readin and writin won't learn you
how to see all they silence in between
My titties ridden by white and black mouths,
my body feeds from womb to tomb to in-between
My silence mistaken for mannered, mild
One day he learned not to test me
Come here, yelled he, *Come here to me clean*

Kerchief goes first, ragged shirt shed
exposin my breasts that fed his mouth
My mistress's old skirt hit the floor
Sun, sky, stars, moon, save me from this doom
I chanted. I cried. Tired arms hugged roun tree
Any named and othas forgotten, you owe me—
change me or give me free. My feet fastened,
I heard first crack, nothin felt pon my hardening back. Started
at my toes, crawled the length of my legs,
arms turned wooded limb, body ripened into widening trunk.
Fingers now branches twisting signs toward sky

My naked bark, kissed by sun
My shadows, my fissures of rage

give no apologies

Scylla and Glaucus at Melrose Hall:
A Cautionary Tale

Prologue

Mi Trut Behind Mi Wall or Last
Will & Testament
Mi mout nuh license wid de church
mi speak di trut in de tongue of mi home

Zimmi?
Nuh tree grow pon mi face Nuhting
mystery in mi looks! 'im a sugamon
son, 'im a risto, 'im nuh resist 'imself

when 'im saw me, 'im became mi man
'im an mi family forced mi to dat place. Mommy,
she obeah like mi gran an mi great gran
When 'im left to dis new place
Mommy sell me to 'im

Fed mi to poison watuhs dem

Mi live mi sweetest years at mi man's feet afta dem a sleep,
'im a wife, 'im picaninny's   dem mi nuh biznizz

'im a gone now, 'im a said 'e go to fight
always 'im a said dis, 'im a said dat while me jungo in 'im
walls. 'im always soon come, soon come
Mi breat thin, mi nuh fool
a shadow of tree treat mi body   mi nuh stay here

I.

At the end of a road, an African woman

Within the pages of literature   She's at Thornfield Hall
                                  This time, her name is Bertha Antoinetta Mason
                                  In otha pages,

they go to her, SHE,
She-Who-Must-Be-Obeyed, Ayesha
Black queen turned white turned ash
turned vapor that could not survive Glaucus's hunger

In America
Loosened from pages and dark places
unfastened from the rock

Black female body hellhound bound   Scylla walks among us
loins now tentacles now arms
reachin into marriage beds
swallowing imaginations

When all disappears,
Black female body remains
For this story, call her Isabella
For this story, she from that dark place

II.

Here, her body reads Black
Here, his beard not encrusted with green
Piscinean features, colossal shoulders,
blue-blooded-sugar-cane-veins in fine threads
Here, Glaucus is cleansed, morality shed   in Gallery 747

Not all robberies are violent   visible
Glaucus   never weaned from Black nipples

found fiendom, salt-water-junkie   Isabella's nipples,
                                     her Mama's nipples,
                                     her Grandmama's nipples…

African woman   Seen
not thirsty nor naked   turned Jamaican christened Black
Glaucus   Some parts God
All sugarcane, all ships   all monster, all more in the new world

III.

Prey and pray in the lap
of Black bodied woman
In the shadow of sugarcane,
Isabella petitions the gods   *Give me, protection*
By shine of the moon, ears of the holy council
pity groans of a grown man,

> I pray you pity a god. Shame forbids me to tell you
> the promises, prayers, and wheeling words I employed
> to be cruelly rejected

When a Black woman rejects a god, a monster
She must pay

Isabella is the cargo
Arriving in the place unnamed
Stolen leads stolen to the tomb
behind the wall above the banquet hall
where time is different

Isabella unseen
    Isabella at his feet
        Isabella, on her knees   Isabella,
                                      Fucked on the floor

                        Isabella,
    Every   pried wide open   disappeared

                                    Behind the wall

IV.

Hide behind the wall   count time different
20 years within hundreds of years
Different versions of hidin   In a kitchen
                            Tucked in a slave shack
                            Secret tunnels in the big house
                            Black woman in every crevice

Glaucus seein Scylla,
white man seein African body
Forever minted concupiscent   there is no question
Black female body   gonna pay the price

Debauched body blamed debauchery
turned crazy bitch in the attic birthed
the side bitch starved to death
hidden behind those walls   The tentacles?

Rabid hellhounds sprout from her bones

V.

In the beginning,
Isabella taken at first sight
lays with He who bathed in 100 rivers
He who bathed in the chants of Neptune
In the beginning,
Isabella lays with the holy   body baptized by poisoned ocean,
                                    sugar cane fields, Melrose Hall

VI.

In the beginning
African woman turned Jamaican blessed Black bodied emerges
entangled in his algae
ends with what they say

A woman from Jamaica
Burst forth, gossamer covered
hair hung to the floor
finger aimed spell spoken   Mi spirit nuh tek yuh
                                Yuh belly swallow yuh

What they say is this was love
What we say is Isabella's truth inked
pon all Black Bodies,

When a white man wants, say yes
When a white man desires,

be prepared to lose your life

VII.

See Glaucus
dissect the threads,
the self-possessed stance,
see the piscenean form

Decipher
West Indian Merchant: Slave Trader
Dark: Black
From Jamaica: A slave from the sugar plantation
Love: Rape

And when you read the version that says she is an Iroquois Princess,
            that says she is the sister-in law who dressed
            in drag to follow him here

they explain why this is a love story

Why   well   we can't cast a full blood negress in this role

Spin The Plate

I neva saw him before that night
he be like no one we eva seen
Richard Green was his name

Tall, slick, dress sharp for these parts
We went to the barn that night to play spin the plate
All the girls buzzed, sheep eye'd sayin,

We neva seen you before
Let's get started fellas holler'd
we fell into place to hear the rules

Spin the plate opposite any clock
If you're called, come step up,
come grab the plate. Don't let it slow. Don't let it drop

I had a feelin I swallowed a snake, goin all night
will be my unmake. Will I make it, will I won't,
I need to be back before massah awakes

Before I knew it, I was up to spin the plate
I took my turn, I closed my eyes callin Richard Green
I felt a burn, I felt the shock, dizziness cloaked me

Richard Green stepped to the center
bringin blasts and bangs unseen
E'body hollar'd as the Sheriff told us to quit it

Richard Green weren't Richard at all
That slicksta-tricksta-lowlife-bandit,
white passin Black tricked us all

I hear Mama screamin and hollerin,
pitchin fuss bout' her baby gone
Life ain't bad in this time-worn barn

Surrounded by jive, talk, and laughter
Richard and I, trapped in this game

Changing Places with the Devil

I allowed this stroll. My stop, his stop
Footfall matched footfall, the moon that night?
Mindin its business, drunk off itself
His skin lit, a bold white like a Magnolia
against corpse quartz threads, a derby hat,
and fresh plucked feather

On the seventh night, he spoke
For your time, your never mind, what's your want?
Gimme, I demand, *your gift of shapeshifting,*
wily wit to trick the world. Make me invincible
in this land of spirits, and gimme...

Mama and Papa warned when want is spoke,
it must be true. Hunger must match crave
Wishin ain't it, but askin will learn ya good
Askin ain't nothing to play wit

Corpse quartz threads line my closet,
A fresh feather plucked for full moon
I've followed a soul for two nights,
weighed the footfalls

It's been found wanting

Ode to the Minotaur

I outbred any bitch
suckle generations at my bosom
My hips, wild for the way I resist name,
I be birthed from Pasiphaë's loins
A Red Buffalo in disguise,
undeclared humanity, my beauty denied
while Venus and Helen forged long lines of Basic Bitches,
passing inheritance of jealousy worthy of Hera
Branding Black bodies with hands, metal or glass
Setting fire to footprints, ripping sun from sky
If only you could

I be the mass
that pinned eyes open to first knowing
causin tongues to writhe with affection
and dispute the indisputable
the original SHE. I snatched your sons,
woo'd your husbands…you wanted to be me
Original theft begetting more theft
I destroyed destruction, unmade your vision
Daedalus's labyrinth requires a globe. Enclosure measured
against height of dread, length of existence
multiplied by a warning from one of your own,
When God awakens to this kind of sin, a reckoning there will be

I be your Moses
Here, you be the god of a land of promise fashioned from found
the god who names what must be contained:
mammy, cook, field hand, wench,
breeder and bred, concubine, no one's wife…
If it can't be contained, consume to become
The way wine is blood, the way crackers be the body
of a divine that neva made you any kind of holy
but birthed anotha kind of whole when one night
lasted 400 years. My name was Plenty and you,
you were Poverty that'd chased me endless

Daedalus couldn't craft a prison big enough to contain the result of that ravishment

Medusa's Otha Sistah, Solitude
or For the Yellow Gal Who Refused

I.

                      to be a good nigger
though history records *La Mulâtresse Solitude,*

(and this part's key)
Light skin, light eyes

could've saved her from what happened to Mama,
from the plantation, from   and...

Rape is not out of the question,
Skin is fair game
Skin is...

II.

                    Skin ain't shit
Wanna know where I'm from follow my skin   follow my skin
                                 from the lightness to light eyes
                                 to the cock of the sailor
                                 that twitched on the slave ship

Papa is Neptune
In anotha place...Hades

Some say Libya birthed me and my sistahs   we really from the interior
only thing, bodies like that?
Really, we needed no temples...really   we been desecrated
No kinky curls fulla venomous snakes

A body bloomed in slick film of runny shit, blood,
             chunks of home that flipped from bellies
             the piss in the hold with stolen cargo
             with the semen that refuses to neatly go
             with the shackles, the screams

Me and mine refuse the future's Hollywood production
as the same kind of motherfucka pried every part of us   open

I cradle vipers in my gut
No name given, I took
No one's half anything
No negress gone wild
of no place.

   I AM SOLITUDE

III.

Tonight, birth no longer
beats against my last breaths
in this shadow of the hangman
I thrust. I instruct:
             Take the name no mortal can give
             Take the freedom no mortal can grant
             Remember, *Resistance to oppression is your natural right*
             Don't forget to have rabbits, one will always escape
             Don't forget, drive a skewer through its body
             with the watchful eye of the oppressor—
             be unafraid to tell them
             This is your fate

Grandmama's vipers,
Mama's vipers,
Now your own
Don't mind your venom,

you are mined from resistance
By sun's rise, Mama's body will hang,
Mama's body will swing in no direction
Postpartum blood will escape my womb

This blood births your siblings. Find them.

IV.

To Find Me...
Resurrection of Solitude:

In some time,
I rise, a body of stone

In some place,
I rise, a body of Iron

Where my body hangs
I am not dead

My soul, your breath
My head, not dismembered
nor snapped nor severed,
like my gaze

Flight From Pygmalion's Pedestal

Appetite tempted into grooming
      resisting sip from ships of open secrets

Those men, those women from that place,
      beauty that defied description bifurcating the tongue

One gave permission for intoxication,
      the other sealing supremacy—Black body foreva ugly

Split tongues wore a claimed Christian thin,
      a concubine or "wife" in this

faraway land won't do. He vowed
      to craft his own. Whip became chisel

Auction block, a sculptor's pedestal
      Plantation turned art studio

Becoming the God of this creation,
      he created a Black woman

in an image within the distortion
      of his own. Hair straight with slightest curl,

a forehead not too high or low
      slight thickened lips, the nose not quite European

Hips not to expand beyond width
      of shoulders. The sculptor molded and sculpted,

blind to the way sun and moon took turns
      to witness audacity of a self-styled Zeus

Giving way to indecision
        Tone of skin, could it be *tawny?* Would it be *copper?*

He settled on *perfectly blacke,*
        strength misshapen for stoicism,

charm and grace fit for self-presumed king,
        and all manner of things misread by male gaze

Within the cradle
        of the world's first superwoman,

completion paired with greedy kiss
        unlocked all *No's.* Firm hands, a reminder of force

Like clay remembers its shape,
        this marble remembered its Creatrix,

this marble refused to wake
        to this slumber. Warmth gave way to blood,

gave way to adrenaline that enlivened feet to flight

Wager:
In Five Acts

ACT I

With moon and stars angled just right
Mama said Massah James called upon his women
Like all us, yuh'll follow this path
Like yuh great gran, gran, n' me, a bed wench yuh'll soon be

This time approachin no different be
'cept mama warned, *Don' get lax, fat, or greedy*
Don' waste a moon on dis doom
Time's drawn near to make use of this month's second moon, rare and blue

Mama said, *A man's urge can't be controll'd*
Be ready cuz time's speed won't slow
Be align'd cuz conjuh n' gods won't wait fuh fools
Mama no longer be but her haint voice still guides me

Follow yuh nose to a biblical flower fuh cleansin, a buckeye fuh new paths
Make cloth dolls of yuh n' Massah James,
form him durin yuh bleedin time, covuh him in dat blood
Wrap yuh doll in his manhood, make all parts switched

Bury these dolls, bury dem deep,
at dat crossin between massah's house and a slave newly birth'd
Hear me close gurl, follow wut I tell yuh
Hear me good, align dis n' yuh'll be free

ACT II

Dis night, he summons me, dis night he says,
My favor'd slave, my best wench, let's play a game, a battle of wit
Let's play for more than priv'leges, food, or trinkets. Let's play for—
Freedom I said, *My Freedom*

He continued to speak like I had not spoke
In the shadows of Solomon and Sheba we shall be
Rounds of riddles from now til dawn
The rules be simple, the rules be plain

First flip of the buckeye declarin who goes first,
anotha flip to tie break. And iffin you best me,
I might grant you stakes higher than my Oak trees… What's your want?
Carryin Mama, gran, and great gran, we knew blankets tatter, extra food spoils

I petition, *Gimme skin fuh skin, rake fuh whip*
Me fuh you, you fuh me, all and whole
Massah chuckled not understandin this no coyness be
This mah only chance, playin fuh keeps it best be

ACT III

This testin of wit seen no end til it was his turn again,
My outside shed, my insides cooked, eaten
I am sometimes placed in bread
My core follows the fate of my skin I dread. What is it gal?

I ansuh'd right and refused to wait
to ax' the one question that'd tangle his tongue
I am the dark half of a full brood
I rise to serve a man most shrewd. Who am I?

Massah laughed, hoot'd, hollarin,
You talkin bout your kind!
No, I said, *these be the djinn under Solomon's command,*
the other half of Adam and Eve's brood, babes abandoned to the night

Anguh invaded his eyes as he announced, *Gal, we be tied*
Mama's haint crept real close plantin whispahs in my ear
She bloomed the words birthed in my throat
Naked and bathed in blue moon, I closed my eyes during this final flip of buckeye

ACT IV

The last step in this conjuh,
the last step to curse my maker's doom,
My skin fuh his skin, my rake fuh his whip
A slave cabin for full plantation. Flesh for flesh. Soul for soul for all generations

NEGRESS! he screamed,
all masculine voice stripped, *Wut's yuh petition to yuh gods done?*
The room chilled, my breasts now flat,
his rose, filled with milk. His lips, swollen with Africa

My nose, European pointed
My lips, thinned. Hips freed from burdens of breedin
Skin of another now skin of another
His new hips gonna bring me many babies

Those hips will keep me and mines fed for generations

ACT V

...and these hands,
oh how firm they grip this whip

BOOK III

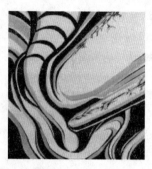

Listen to the elders, for it is wisdom
Listen to the ancestors, for it is survival
Heed the words of the long dead

They are warning shots

Tituba's Last Words

Stolen body?
Stolen land?
Of course I did it

What did you think was going to happen?

Name Not…
A Conversation

Funny, finding a place never lost, already named,
there's nothing new about me

The christening and naming
of a body never misplaced

I was a turtle's back longer
  than I was a mapmaker's namesake,

Mama's somewhere,
  she calls me by my secret names

a united anything, somebody's idea
of a new world

Dismemberment and outright stealing
the way "discovery" became an idea turned lust

They think I have their amnesia,
        their forgetting…

Something about us,
████████ inviting █████████…

I am millions,
        not hundreds old

Lessons from Daedalus and Icarus
as told by the Igbo at Igbo's landing

*'...King Minos can block
my escape,
by land or water,' he signed. 'The air, at least, is still open;
my path lies there. He is lord of the world, but not lord of
the sky.'*

Book 8, Daedalus and Icarus, *Metamorphoses*

Our wings,
never wax or feathered
They be of will
Freedom's not given nor taken
by earthly souls

He be no lord

Of no world, no sky, no water,
and thus, no body
Us?
Never to be placed in this maze
called America

They gonna say

it never happened despite one witness
We needed no permission
You still asking where?
Most known things be marked beyond what they tell you

Queen Ranavalona's Commandments for the Way Back

Silent observation   not agreement
     but the way back

1. Undo any agreements with the colonizers.
2. Untwist your tongue from their speak.
3. Unlearn their symbols, create your own.
4. Use their tools, use their knowledge,
   dismantle their house.
5. Find the footsteps of those you belong to,
   follow them.
6. Build a mirage of simplicity.
7. Get their Gods out of your veins, rinse their prayers from your mouth.
8. Guard your natural resources,
   you'll know what they are.
9. Become all and none of what they say.
   Be the wild they fear.
10. For the ones you trust, test them with poison.
    For the ones you trust, they will survive this ordeal.

Be and do all the things and the things they'll accuse

I am Queen of an island, but you...
You are a sovereign of self.

Philomela's Tapestry Speaks
for African-American girl nude, reclining on couch c.1882

"But suffering sharpens the wit and misfortune makes one
resourceful.
She craftily strung a warp on a primitive Thracian loom,
and into pure white threads she wove a message in purple
letters revealing the crime."

Book 6, Tereus, Procne, and Philomela, *Metamorphoses*

I am my master's tongue imprinted
      upon the palimpsest of what is

Read me close…arm framing immature hips
      that refuse to speak the fluent language of fucking

No nipple nor breast upturned
      to kiss light, no divan, but reclined on couch

Maybe she be Grand or Reclining Odalisque,
      Venus of Urbino, Olympia

They ain't kin to me
      My freedom neva sounded like dat

Hair as is, as if having
      been scooped from a braider's hands. Crafted and fit

for no museum, instead for
      hands. Somewhere between care, curiosity,

Where's her mama?, and judgement standing
      upon nameless as foundation, as

if landscapes built by amnesiacs
	threaten to suck even this language from me

This was that hour Satan,
	a chaperone, a guardian, a parent,

or photographer's wife couldn't
	prevent this body from being stamped

nor hid from labored breath between damage,
	a hard prick, sickness, the glare of white gaze

The way the stench
	of desperation claims parts unknown

The way a draft, a strange
	place, and albumen wraps a naked body

Come close enough to chase the
	girlhood that hovers on the borrowed time

of She-Who-Is-Woman-Disguised-As-Girl,
	Fading-From-View. Dignity held, necked popped steel-stiff

despite awkward configuration and lips
	refusing passage sayin,

Imma let you think you can take this
	Eyes adding punctuation

Tapestry instructions for care:

Read between time, appear the missing
Read unwanted, bargained

Follow the loops over and under
Age 220 years

Take me out of the archive. Place me in the open
Let your tongue go missing

How to Reverse a Conjure
   —for Remus

Owl's blood?
Too easy
Easy like the way
you appeared
and disappeared life
That kinda power always
has balance

When you and yours
want to be Gods,
know that even Gods must
observe the rules:
No buried jars facing East
under no flowering tree
No owls killed by human hands

This kind of undoing requires…

Nat Turner's Wisdom

A fanatic for the way I knew: blood on corn —
heaven's dew, the way earth spun, the shift in
seasons. For the way I read time tellin, *Masters
can be slayed with their own tools.* I tended my garden
of death, pruning begot pruning, yet,
I brought back the memory of berserk. Monster?
My skin, familial keepsakes. Fat from body
now oil and soap, all eternal reminders posing
the question: Who's the real monster?
Who's the obsessed, true berserker?
When God, a moment, or vision says gimme,
from scalp to toenail, skin to bones, be ready!
Risks demand surrender of self-whole, faith
beyond prayer. Taking what is decreed at birth?
It was always mines. As for when?

Don't let anyone tell you now isn't it

BOOK IV

Dey said if somethin lost and don't come back,
it ain't meant

They don't know such thangs

Like they don't know my bones,
my bones   they dowse, they divine

They don't know...

The same They also said the broken stay broken,

But they broken ain't my broken
They know nothin of my salve

Black Soul: A Short Story Abo▮▮▮▮▮▮▮▮
Volume 1

Tereus, Procne, and Philomela's Children (Part II)

It wasn't so much about Disney
        but the way a frame encases a Black

grandson telling his grandfather, "Look
        – I brought you with me and brought it back…see"

No, that's not it. It was the way hands
        collided with air. The way we knew to read

between the fingers becoming words
        becoming the real message he tells grandpa,

"You never left"

As far as signs go, we it.
But as far as signs go,

Necessity is only miraculous
        when it can be taken and hung

All of us left to think we're in on it
        The way the curator's tags,

titles, and sometimes, docents think they
        create a bridge to something. What were

their names? What were their lives
        beyond the fabric of Gee's Bend?

What was it they were saying,
in cheerleader's costumes?

Tranced out Latinx sitting around a
table. The crook, bend, arch of fingers,

of elbows becoming the gravity
lifting gold pieces from their necks.

Americana with the flava
of straight up gang members. All

of us encased in Dartmouth's Hood. We've
arrived, except I'd keep returning

to the head of the table, open-
eyed, empty of the uniform, the gold,

and the signs. Except, I'd be the one haunted
knowing y'all were in on it.

It would take a certain kind of life math
to pierce the seventeen years

Unbroken burden, the blaze upon her skin
No need to ever touch to know this

ain't caution. It be danger. Mama's
words spat fast plus the 26 years to

read the white space. Not enough to
equal the family secret. I settle for

trying to find my face in the cut
of great-grandma's cheekbones trying to read

her eyes as she stood in front of me once
as an introduction amid my bound tongue

and arms too weak to lift the why that
        formed. That resin coated over us,

my awkward arm giving the only
        hug its allowed to give, and a smile

full of no knowing. The next time,
        I'd see you through a screen. This time,

your face wears the same stoicism
        imprinted between cheekbones

erected upon a steel spine
        All child's gaze gone, I pick apart

the pieces in a wordless riddle

                        questions fluent in woman...
                                I finally know what it was about

That boy and his grandfather, trading
        signs adding to my well of want

They got it in the way Procne could
        read Philomela. The way I knew that

in this version, I'm Procne reading
        the loops and stitches of this cloth

still deciphering the maze of symbols.
        And sometimes, I'm left with that kind of

lust that makes me Tereus
        The kind that makes me want to cut out a tongue to learn

to speak its truth

Blessed Black

or is it African American, Neosoul Love Jones finger snap negro,
or is it blessed my nigga from around the way, or the new negro
sprung from the loins of Zora, Countee, Langston, Augusta,
Billie n' dem. Maybe fam, cuz, brotha, sista...

Legend says the Dutch
were trynna say from Niger
others blame Latin

All we know
is from the spray
from spittle of white mouths

like a Circean wand,
we be blesstized Black

Back in the day *Birth of a Nation* be our Gorgon, Black bodies
turned stone in America's gaze. Dangerous, good for nothin, lazy...
then who the hell built all this? Here, the Obamas rivaled the Huxtables
rivaled the Jeffersons rivaled Good Times, movin on up uppity...
careful, they can't believe we wanna be above our colah, venture beyon
station of skin. Back in the day, all that causin white rage: 1923 Rosewood,
the 1919 Red Summer that reigned three seasons, 1917 East St. Louis,
1906 Atlanta, 1834 Philly's flying horses, all the ways they say,
We been doin this

Applying Ovid's
Pythagorean theory:
Black bodies shapeshift

Shape and shift, neva bucks, neva wenches, nobody's stud, notchya
mammy, pickaninny, jezebel, nobody's wedding gift, nobody's inheritance.
Defiled mulatto and yellow, tainted quadroon, octoroon, all shades
of names for massa-got-him-some. Simply put, rape-colored
Unbranded *good natur'd, good temper'd*

Unmade *stout, nobody's sturdy, able, straight limb'd…*
What we really sayin is, *'These here, they reeealll valuable.'*
Maybe be like Black hair, that natural, rice water grown fully weaned
from that whack creamy crack, that loosen the curl chemical, no more
faux natural. No more prayin to the God of Good Hair, good hair's cancelled,
no nostrils filled with the sizzle of Blue Magic kissin hot combs, no more
askin to be like Myra, Ebony, Toya, Lisa, those girls, any girl with that
good hair. Maybe be like forgettin the word that rhymed with happy,
Droppin happy, droppin kinky, droppin coils altogetha. And for
the record, nobody's boxer braids, but once-coded-for-freedom-
corn-rows

Tignon laws told us
they been policin our bodies
legal shades n' cadavers

became the mistake
meant for a sewin machine
turned test on dog's fur

It was really Madam C.J. preachin
Let your crown glory be

…is it Black as in river-bed-Black, Bedouin Brown,
Deep-Chocolate-Alek-Wek-Brown, Sahara Brown,
Red Bone as in fine as in Light Skin, Cinnamon,
Sugar- Cookie-Slightly-Burnt as in Caramel, Ginger Snap.
Maybe Trail-of-Tears under-tones like Rose Gold hue
Hershey's Kiss, far, far away from plantation as in
massa-ain't-touch-none-of-this. We-need-a-new-name-to-describe-that-kind, the noth-
ing-added-to-that-epidermis, nothing added to dare reflect any other color

Offensively-uncategorized-Black

or is it Blaque, Blaq, POC,
is it BIPOC,
not colored but of some color

is it   ?
                     ?
                     ?

Original names? We know nothin. We be the
Unnamed,
      Nonamed
            Renamed

Poisonwell Diaries:
Psalms of the Ossuary

I.

My mouth holds ungloved
hands while I sit in a chair
as a pale Latina
hums her "We" in my ear when
white invades a sentence

She is the *they* I can't unsee

II.

I am mine only
when permission is granted
Permission is granted
to lay on his table   His
excitement and my Black

body fills the room
This body is solid, and
these hips...these hips are
built for babies   He taught
his sons to travel the world

III.

This time, we ride an
open train car somewhere in
India an English
accent wraps my body
along with instruction:

To the white man who snagged
a Black one, *What are you waiting for?*

IV.

Beget the children,
she's made for it

My ears ring
with Bigbone eyes holding
the smile of a lightskin
dude time travelin like Papa,

He carries us to
another there   He's
the master's son   Here
he plans my future I am to
be with him

I am to be his cook

V.

Some part of each day
Mama and me stuck in a
bedroom   I am the
cute to her beautiful   She
continues tellin me what

I am and what I am not

VI.

Some part of the night
I return to that dance floor
where white hands touch, forceful
grip   She, explainin why she
just had to   Me losin count

of the unnamed they
of the way need and apology
are a snake's open mouth
never aware of
devouring its own tail

VII.

My feet stay in stirrups
My body holds a cold
rod and unwarned gloved
fingers   I cause annoyance
I cause White Coat's questions that
demand answers,

In that place, did someone touch you?
In that place, did someone force you?
In that place, you do not behave
You do not stay still

VIII.

Those voices?   Them
explainin me to myself
remindin me   I'm an
undocked ghost ship. I'm an
ossuary of the unknown

awakening fingers
to their poke, to their prod,
and the eyes that
remember how to twist tongues
into language askin...

How much?

The Return of Hyena Man

She barely escaped him once
shifting from tree to water to stone

to something else—

No one knew it but Hyena Man had a brother
No one knew it but Hyena Man had a whole den
just like him
Now that that he knew there were others like her,
a pack of them would be back

The sun at its highest, the sky cerulean wiped clean of clouds
The gods blessed this day good. She told Mama, she told Papa
she'd soon be far from here. Within a few hours the whole village
knew she'd be going far, far away from here
In the middle of celebration,
Mama needed the details. Amid the sounds
of giddy-senseless-happy,
Mama demanded her to tell

I have land, just come with me
I have riches, come with me
No problem traveling across the sea, I have ships,
come be with me
No won't be an answer,
you won't say no, I know you won't
but let's say you did
I'd still take you away
I'd take you far
I need the world to see my catch

Mama,
I told him I'd become so strong and tall
extend my roots far from his reach
So sturdy and wide I'd be
His shadow and all like him would be swallowed by me

I'll let you grow tall, then cut you down
Grow you so tall, you'd kiss the sun
I'd cut you down and sand you smooth
You'll become a chest of drawers,
the countertop in my kitchen forever bound

What would be next for you?

Mama,
I said I'd become the most poisonous plant
Poison to taste, wicked to touch and smell
He wouldn't be able to get near me

I've trained in poison my whole life
I'll chew you and swallow you,
swallow you whole
Afterwards, there'd be nothing of you
And what if I am taking you to the place where I am world?
Where I am deity?

Mama,
I...

You've tasted the honey of his words   it is too late
I can't save you from this fate. You are headed to Jangare
Child be quiet, child be still
and mine this time,
for time will soon go missing

Child be quiet. Child be still
I'll show you where Gods go to die
and this one...

He's no god
He's the thief who has come to take you from me

BOOK V

Rage is the justified anger of the righteous
Blood, it splatters into places unseen and upon hands that don't directly butcher

Dust knows nothin of settlin

And the land?
It hasn't stopped beating against itself to teach us how to listen

I. America and Europe

I am
only because you took
you erased my age,
my people

We gave you our rejects
You eat our unwanted gods

You be our dumping ground

II.   America and Africa

Like everything else,
They came   *Like them, you hunger*
They saw   *you became infected*
They took…   *Like them, you tried to eat all my…*
and took

As much as they took   *You devoured my people*
I am the land of barren   *became impregnated with my memory*
of stolen,   *parts of me live in your bones*
not promise

How can I eat you as you say, devour as you say
what was thrust upon me?

I didn't ask for this
To be solace for greed
Host of wayward children
running from royal papas

Understand,
like you, I just was
until they renamed me
Understand,
I had to do what they wanted
when they came

                                   Millions-years-old you say?
                                   A toddler still learning words I say

                                   There is no numeric value
                                   that could be placed upon my body…
                                   I am beginning of everything

III. Europe and America

My name
for the way it means wide
like my appetite

> *I may be the dumping ground,*
> *paradise for the wayward, but you…*
> *you brought Hunger into my belly*

How did I become the girl
kidnapped by a God?

> *There's a price to pay for taking*
> *May your hunger drive you to your own end*
> *May you have no choice*
> *but to eat yourselves*

I had to remind the world
I am the God,
not the girl
I am the once wild that refused taming
I was…

> *May you never be the god,*
> *but the girl*
> *Always the girl kept and trapped*
> *by gilded cage as home stays missing*
> *Your memory of what was,*
> *what you take will leave you,*
> *like this…*

IV. A Note from Africa to Europe

What came first Europa or you?
Granted you can call yourself "Old World"
Like a child, you forget whose you are,
who you belong to

Cradle as in cave as in Mama's womb
Mamas must be ready for babes to burn their cradles
As you set the fire, you tried to take my limbs
As you set the fire, you took what you called your inheritance

I still have my head. I still have my neck
I turn in every direction…I see all

You are what you've eaten, what you've taken
Since you've eaten my children,
many children from other places,
swallowed my stories, stolen so many tongues,

Who are you without all of us?

V. Africa's Interrogatories to America

Do you remember your name
your children gave you before they came?
Do you remember the shape of your body,
the rise and fall of your bosom, how no part of you

was beholden to any man,
let alone self-made sovereignty?
Do you remember your face before they changed it?
Show me what you were before they made you forget
Do you remember the realm of your belly
before they made you imbibe upon bodies?

Do you remember taste before your tongue
was trained in blood?
Do you remember...

      What you are?

      Who you are?

      Now that you've forgotten,
      what do you want to be?

      What will you be child, what will you be
      now that you've mimicked your kidnappers
      continuing to take so many parts of me?

Coda: Origin Story

Stealing sprouts intimacy
foundation laid for contagion
I am devoured
I am thirst unquenched

Coordinates lost to Mama's
I've memorized every room in your house
I built the blueprint

I am Mitochondrial Eve
squat wide in day's death
and I am the child retracing
buried placenta

I am sister to Atunda,
He-who-broke-and-birthed-Gods
I knew you were comin

Through tongue through eyes
through ears I entered
Through pores of skin
I am your interior, your fever eternal

You saw,
you opened wide
cause you knew you'd become

I won't travel you ragged
Won't twist and tear your tongue
Gimme your children

         I'm takin your children

Your appetite groomed me,
          grew me up

That hunger? Thirst? Lust? Want?   ?
          ?   ? And   ?

There is no language,
no alphabet contains what
Imma do to you

NOTES

Erysichthon's Seed
This poem includes a reference from the story of a Kentucky slave owner, Lilburn Lewis, who told his wife that he'd never had as much fun at a ball as he did that evening he chopped up one of his slaves. The full story in context shared within *The Delectable Negro* by Vincent Woodard (2014).

Tereus, Procne, and Philomela's Children (Part I)
The redacted section of this poem is taken from the article, "The battle to get Europe to return thousands of Africa's stolen artifacts is getting complicated," by Ciku Kimeria on Quartz.com which can be seen in the following link: qz.com/africa/1758619/europes-museums-are-fighting-to-keep-africas-stolen-artifacts/

Echo's Revenge
I went to Salem, Massachusetts for the first time in late fall 2019. While there, I visited the Peabody Essex Museum which had an exhibition about the intermingling of desire as linked to power, imperialism, opium wars, trade, and current opioid related deaths. You can see more about this exhibition by visiting: Pem.org/blog/every-eleven-minutes.

If You End Up in Jangare: An Incantation for Remembering
Inspired by an African myth cited in *A Dictionary of African Mythology: The Mythmaker as Storyteller* by Harold Scheub (2000).

The Witness Tree
While reading from many narratives within the Federal Writers' Project, 1936-1938, there were many interesting stories shared by individuals formerly enslaved. One item was a phrase, "Come to me clean," as shared by a woman known as Aunt Ferebe Rogers as she talked about the ways that enslaved individuals were abused by their masters on plantations. This story can be seen in full in Georgia, Volume 4, Part 1 in the interview titled "Aunt Ferebe Rogers, Baldwin County, Milledgeville, GA."

Scylla and Glaucus at Melrose Hall: A Cautionary Tale
The quote from part III of the poem is a direct quote from Glaucus within Ovid's *Metamorphoses*, Book 14, pp. 548-9

Spin the Plate
This poem is inspired by an account of a story shared by Josephine Anderson of an individual possibly trying to pass for Black and killed in a shootout while at a gathering of African Americans playing a game of spin the plate taken from the Federal Writers' Project: Slave Narrative Project, Vol. 3, Florida, Anderson-Wilson (with combined interviews of others). The full story and interview with Josephine Anderson can be accessed by going to: https://www.loc.gov/resource/mesn.030/?sp=5

Changing Place with the Devil
This poem is inspired by what Josephine Anderson shared about walking home one night when she was asked about ghosts and haints taken from the Federal Writers' Project: Slave Narrative Project, Vol. 3, Florida, Anderson-Wilson (with combined interviews of others). The full story and interview with Josephine Anderson can be accessed by going to: https://www.loc.gov/resource/mesn.030/?sp=5

Flight from Pygmalion
Includes the references from early reports of visitors to Africa.

Philomela's Tapestry Speaks
This is an ekphrastic poem based on the Tomas Eakins photograph, "African-American girl nude, reclining on couch." This photograph is also discussed at length in Dr. Saidiya Hartman's book, *Wayward Lives, Beautiful Experiments: Intimate Histories of Riotous Black Girls, Troublesome Women, and Queer Radicals* (2019).

How to Reverse a Conjure
Inspired by a story about an enslaved man named Remus who was beaten to death by his enslaver. The enslaver ordered a chest to be built and was not satisfied with the chest thus, beating Remus to his death. More about this chest that has plagued generations of the Graham family can be read here: History.ky.gov/2019/10/30/new-details-about-the-cursed-chest/

Blessed Black
Includes references from ads created by enslavers.

The Return of the Hyena Man
This poem was inspired by the Ghanian story, "Tale of the Girl and the Hyena-Man" within the book, *Beauty and the Beast: Classic Tales About Animal Brides and Grooms from Around the World* by Maria Tatar.

Illustrations in Black Metamorphoses by Alan Blackwell
The images that appear in this collection are a part of a full set of 13 images created for the manuscript.

"Poisonwell Diaries: The Ghost" was created based on the poem with the same name within the *Black Metamorphoses* collection. The original print is 14" x 20" done using ink and brush techniques.

"Mandala" was created to represent the whole experience of *Black Metamorphoses*. The original print is 14" x 20" using ink and brush techniques.

"Philomela's Tapestry Speaks" was created based on the poem, "Philomela's Tapestry Speaks for African-American girl nude, reclining on couch c. 1882, " within the *Black Metamorphoses* collection. The original print is 14" x 20" using ink and brush techniques.

"Tereus, Procne, and Philomela's Children" was created based on the poems "Tereus, Procne, and Philomela's Children" parts 1 and 2. This image is also the cover for *Black Metamorphoses*. The original print is 14" x 20" using ink and brush techniques.

"Erysichthon's Seed" was created based on the poem by the same name within the *Black Metamorphoses* collection. The original print is 14" x 20" using ink and brush techniques.

About The Author

Shanta Lee is a writer of poetry, creative nonfiction, journalism, a visual artist and public intellectual actively participating in the cultural discourse with work that has been widely featured. She is also the creator and producer of Vermont Public's "Seeing... the Unseen and In-Between within Vermont's Landscape" and is a regular contributor to *Ms. Magazine* and Art New England. Shanta Lee is also the author of the poetry collection, *GHETTOCLAUSTROPHOBIA: Dreamin of Mama While Trying to Speak Woman in Woke Tongues*, winner of the 2020 Diode Editions full-length book prize and the 2021 Vermont Book Award. Within this latest illustrated poetry collection, *Black Metamorphoses* (Etruscan Press, 2023) is a work that Shanta Lee describes as a 2,000+ year-old phone line opened to Ovid as well as an interrogation of the Greek mythos while creating her own new language in this work. *Black Metamorphoses* has been named a finalist in the 2021 Hudson prize, shortlisted for the 2021 Cowles Poetry Book Prize and longlisted for the 2021 Idaho poetry prize. Shanta Lee is the 2020 recipient of the Arthur Williams Award for Meritorious Service to the Arts and 2020 and the 2020 gubernatorial appointee to the Vermont Humanities Council's board of directors. Her current multimedia exhibition, *Dark Goddess: An Exploration of the Sacred Feminine*, which features her short film, interviews, and photography, and other items has been on view University of Vermont's Fleming Museum of Art and the Southern Vermont Arts Center. Shanta Lee has an MFA in Creative Non-Fiction and Poetry from the Vermont College of Fine Arts, an MBA from the University of Hartford and an undergraduate degree in Women, Gender and Sexuality from Trinity College.

Across all of her endeavors, Shanta Lee shares, "I have an enduring passion and hunger to explore the unseen and invite others into that space of inquiry. What is someone's story under the surface of their face and presentation? What is forgotten to human memory that should be reclaimed? Or, most simply, how can I share the sense or soul of a place with someone who may not ever travel there? This endless hunger to ask questions, create conversation through visual or written commentary, and journey into the unknown through my various creative endeavors or collaborations thrives even if what I unearth scares me."

To learn more about her work, visit: Shantalee.com.

About the Illustrator

Alan Blackwell, studied drawing and painting at SUNY Purchase College in New York. He paints using ink and brush in stylized and repetitive brushstrokes to invoke subtleties of movement and imagery. While having a deep appreciation for calligraphy and fine brush work, Alan is also the product of comic books and graphic novels. His studies as an artist has included his time with a calligraphy master in China. He currently lives in Southern Vermont with his family. Of his work, Alan shares, "I have a singular goal when people view my artwork. I hope that the viewer will be able to see something unique to themselves. This can mean the slightest suggestion of a face or figure, a convergence of brush strokes, or perhaps a reversal of foreground and background. Flowing forms and repetitive brush strokes help to create a uniquely inviting environment. Stark contrasts and smooth edges create worlds whose depths I love to explore."

Books from Etruscan Press

Zarathustra Must Die | Dorian Alexander
The Disappearance of Seth | Kazim Ali
The Last Orgasm | Nin Andrews
Drift Ice | Jennifer Atkinson
Crow Man | Tom Bailey
Coronology | Claire Bateman
Reading the Signs and other itinerant essays | Stephen Benz
Topographies | Stephen Benz
What We Ask of Flesh | Remica L. Bingham
The Greatest Jewish-American Lover in Hungarian History | Michael Blumenthal
No Hurry | Michael Blumenthal
Choir of the Wells | Bruce Bond
Cinder | Bruce Bond
The Other Sky | Bruce Bond and Aron Wiesenfeld
Peal | Bruce Bond
Scar | Bruce Bond
Poems and Their Making: A Conversation | Moderated by Philip Brady
Crave: Sojourn of a Hungry Soul | Laurie Jean Cannady
Toucans in the Arctic | Scott Coffel
Sixteen | Auguste Corteau
Wattle & daub | Brian Coughlan
Body of a Dancer | Renée E. D'Aoust
Generations: Lullaby with Incendiary Device, The Nazi Patrol, and How It Is That We |
Dante Di Stefano, William Heyen, and H. L. Hix
Ill Angels | Dante Di Stefano
Aard-vark to Axolotl: Pictures From my Grandfather's Dictionary | Karen Donovan
Trio: Planet Parable, Run: A Verse-History of Victoria Woodhull, and Endless Body |
Karen Donovan, Diane Raptosh, and Daneen Wardrop
Scything Grace | Sean Thomas Dougherty
Areas of Fog | Will Dowd
Romer | Robert Eastwood
Wait for God to Notice | Sari Fordham
Surrendering Oz | Bonnie Friedman
Nahoonkara | Peter Grandbois
Triptych: The Three-Legged World, In Time, and Orpheus & Echo |
Peter Grandbois, James McCorkle, and Robert Miltner
The Candle: Poems of Our 20th Century Holocausts | William Heyen

Etruscan Press Is Proud of Support Received From

Wilkes University

Youngstown State University

Ohio Arts Council

The Stephen & Jeryl Oristaglio Foundation

Community of Literary Magazines and Presses

National Endowment for the Arts

Drs. Barbara Brothers & Gratia Murphy Endowment

The Thendara Foundation

Founded in 2001 with a generous grant from the Oristaglio Foundation, Etruscan Press is a nonprofit cooper-ative of poets and writers working to produce and promote books that nurture the dialogue among genres, achieve a distinctive voice, and reshape the literary and cultural histories of which we are a part.

Etruscan Press
www.etruscanpress.org

Etruscan Press books may be ordered from

Consortium Book Sales and Distribution
800.283.3572
www.cbsd.com

Etruscan Press is a 501(c)(3) nonprofit organization.
Contributions to Etruscan Press are tax deductible
as allowed under applicable law.
For more information, a prospectus,
or to order one of our titles,
contact us at books@etruscanpress.org.